HUNGARIAN FOLK DESIGNS

For Embroiderers and Craftsmen

Anne Szalavary

Dover Publications, Inc.
New York

DEDICATION
For my husband Joe, with love.

Published in Canada by General Publishing Company, Ltd., 30 Lesmill Road, Don Mills, Toronto, Ontario.
Published in the United Kingdom by Constable and Company, Ltd.

Hungarian Folk Designs for Embroiderers and Craftsmen is a new work, first published by Dover Publications, Inc., in 1980.

DOVER *Pictorial Archive* SERIES

International Standard Book Number: 0-486-23969-1
Library of Congress Catalog Card Number: 79-57220

Manufactured in the United States of America
Dover Publications, Inc.
180 Varick Street
New York, N.Y. 10014

Introduction

In its purest form, folk art is the hand creation of a utilitarian object and its embellishment with traditional designs. Folk art reflects the taste and culture of people living in small villages and on isolated farms; it has always been a working-class phenomenon—kept alive by artisans and small tradesmen pursuing their livelihoods in peasant communities. The methods and motifs are handed down from generation to generation, century to century, both in actual samples and in written records. Historical background, economic status, climate and geography all play important parts in both the selection of the designs and in the final execution of the work in the chosen medium, be it needlework, woodcarving, painting, and so forth.

Nowhere are the traditions of folk art better preserved and amplified than in Hungary. The Hungarian folk artist's use of furniture, dwelling places, bedclothes, festive and everyday garments, pottery and interior decor can be compared to the fine artist at his easel creating a masterpiece on plain canvas. Hungarian folk art vividly expresses the Magyar temperament; one can almost hear the strains of the gypsy violins and see the flashing, whirling czardas in the flamboyant array of colors.

You can add an authentic touch of Hungarian flavor to your own embroidery and crafts through the use of the designs in this collection. All these motifs have been developed and adapted from old Hungarian folk embroidery designs acquired in Hungary by my mother.

Hungarian folk art designs are a field of study unto themselves. Through the centuries, the various regions of the country have developed not only their own motifs and designs, but also their own traditional ways of embroidering them. Thus the patterns in this collection are organized alphabetically by geographical area, and each region's work is introduced by a short note giving information on characteristic themes, color schemes and stitches. Although there are many more districts in Hungary with beautiful and distinctive design traditions, the thirteen I have chosen give a good overview of Hungarian folk design. The accompanying map shows each area's location within the country.

As a general rule, Hungarian folk art embroidery features stylized plants and flowers—tulips, poppies, cornflowers, carnations, forget-me-nots, daisies, marigolds, lilies-of-the-valley and many more. These are the basic designs from which the regional artists evolve their distinctive creations. While certain color schemes and motifs may be traditional within a community, each artist strives to add his own personal touch to each piece. The work thus becomes an authentic handmade original and not a mere copy of historic work. Each generation makes some small contribution, thereby constantly renewing the cultural heritage.

In somewhat similar fashion, you should feel free to combine motifs and methods from two or more regions. A flower from here, a leaf from there, and you're on your way to making something old yet new, traditional yet personal.

TRANSFERRING THE DESIGNS

Step 1. Gather the materials needed for transferring.

You will need:
Tracing paper
Large piece of cardboard (oak tag or tablet back)
Straight pins
Tracing wheel, dull pencil or other stylus
Ruler
Dressmaker's carbon paper (in a color that contrasts with the color of the fabric)
Flat smooth surface (such as a table)
Background fabric

Step 2. Make a tracing by putting a sheet of tracing paper over the design and drawing over each line with a lead pencil. We do not advise tracing directly from the book onto the fabric because the page might tear and render the designs on the overleaf page unusable.

Step 3. Transfer the design. Place the cardboard on a flat surface; this not only protects the surface of the table from scarring under the pressure of the tracing wheel but also provides the firm padding under the fabric necessary to produce a smooth line. Carefully position your tracing on the fabric and pin it at the four corners. If the design is to be centered, use a ruler to determine the midpoint.

Before we proceed with the transfer process, let me say a word about carbon papers. Do *not* use typewriter carbon; it will smudge and rub off on the fabric and is almost impossible to remove. Dressmaker's carbon, available at notions, fabric and dime stores, comes in packs of assorted colors in strips about 7 × 20 inches. It has a hard waxy finish and is designed for our purpose.

Slip the carbon, color-side down, between the tracing and the fabric, temporarily removing one of the corner pins if necessary. Do not pin the carbon in place. If you place the pins through the carbon, you will end up with unsightly splotches on your fabric.

With a hard, even pressure, trace a few lines with a tracing wheel or similar tool. Raise one corner of the tracing and the carbon to check the impression. If the results are too faint, apply more pressure; if too heavy, less pressure. Too heavy a line is difficult to hide with embroidery and too light a line is hard to see, but keep in mind that the transfer does have a tendency to fade a bit as it is handled and so should be a little on the heavy side. After adjusting the impression, trace the entire design and then remove the carbon and all but two pins. Carefully lift one side of the tracing paper and check to make sure the design is intact on the fabric *before removing the pattern*. Once removed it is almost impossible to register the pattern to the fabric again.

If later on, during the embroidery process, the line becomes too faint, touch it up with a waterproof felt-tip pen or a laundry marker. Test the pen! If it is not waterproof it will run and ruin your embroidery; just the moisture from a steam iron is enough to cause this. (A pencil can be used unless you are working with light-colored yarns which the lead could discolor.)

MATERIALS

At first, the only material available in Hungary for all types of needlework was the rough homespun linen made from hemp (*kender*) and flax (*len*) that was used for all clothing and household linens. Recent modernization and new techniques now give embroiderers in Hungary and the world over a wide array of beautiful blends and synthetics from which to choose. Fabric selection has become very much a question of personal preference. Linens of many weights, cottons, tweeds, velvets, corduroys and the many synthetics available are all equally suitable. There is only one stipulation: be sure to follow closely the instructions on pattern envelopes as to the material best suited for the item of clothing you intend to sew. The pattern company's advice is the best rule of thumb. If, however, you wish to decorate ready-made clothes, you have only to choose the pattern and colors preferred in working them. At any rate, check the label before purchasing to make sure the material is preshrunk. Ask your salesclerk for assistance in this area for there is nothing more annoying than completing a great piece of needlework and finding that after washing, the stitches are all lumped up because the material has shrunk. So be sure to preshrink those fabrics which need it before embarking on your transfer and embroidery work. After completing your work, place it right side down on a padding of thick terry towelling and steam press lightly using a damp cloth and a medium hot iron. Leave the work to dry completely before handling.

I find the commercial six-strand embroidery floss easier to handle than the various cotton threads which are available. It is best, however, to experiment with different types until you find the one that performs to your satisfaction.

MAP OF HUNGARY SHOWING CRAFT DISTRICTS

Stitches

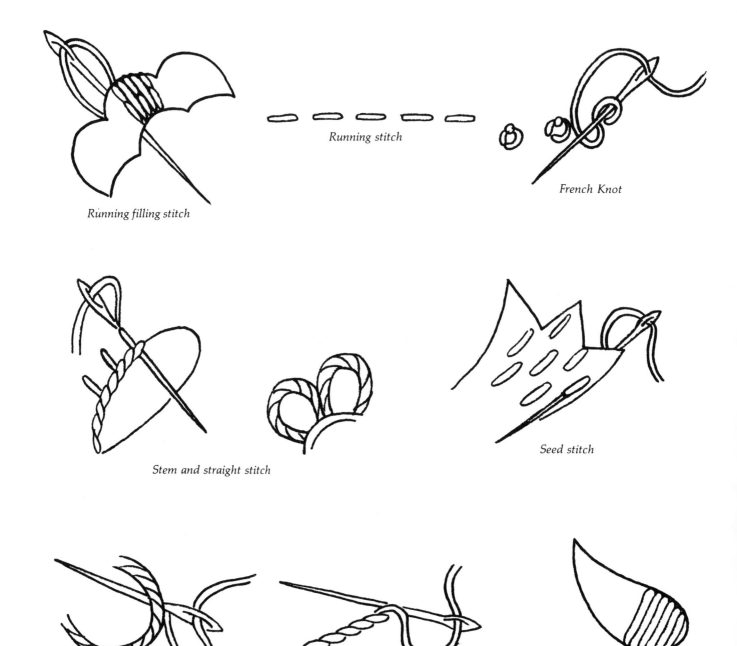

Running filling stitch

Running stitch

French Knot

Stem and straight stitch

Seed stitch

Stem or outline stitch

Satin stitch

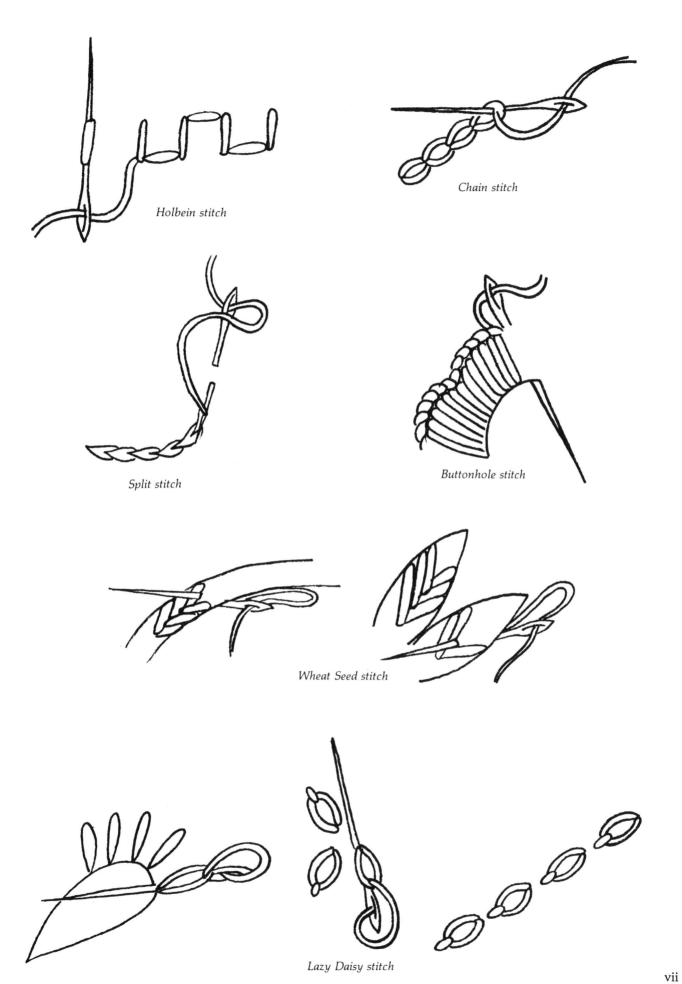

Holbein stitch

Chain stitch

Split stitch

Buttonhole stitch

Wheat Seed stitch

Lazy Daisy stitch

The Alföld

The three regions of Hódmezővásárhely, Kunság and Békés make up the Alföld or lowland area of Hungary. The colors in Alföld embroidery range from pink to red, beige to brown, pale green to avocado, with touches of black for accent.

In the Alföld, satin stitch is traditionally used for working flowers, leaves, buds and zigzag filling. Lazy daisy stitches are used to do stylized petal details while vine detailing and flower and leaf outlines are worked in stem stitch. Wheat seed stitch is usually used for stems and star-flower shapes.

Baranya & Bacsmegye

The embroidery of the Baranya and Bacsmegye area uses red, white, black, yellow, blue, brown, golden yellow and various brown hues. In addition, blues from light to dark; combinations of red—blue-brown; red—blue—black; white on white, and shades of gold are all used to work the lively designs.

Traditionally vines, leaf and flower outlines are worked in stem stitch. Satin stitch is used for filling leaves, flowers and petals and running stitch for leaf filling variations. Square details are worked in Holbein stitch with seed or French knots for filling leaves and flowers.

This area also produces the exquisite szúr work, consisting of delicately cut and appliquéd felt scroll work in a variety of dtsigns and colors. Red, black and white are just some of the colors that are combined for attractive adornments on jackets, vests, tablecloths and pillowcases.

For a successful szúr work project, it is important to choose a medium-weight felt with a smooth, even weave, because the cutting and handling of the finer parts of the design tend to pull apart the material. Trace the design of your choice and transfer it to the article you wish to decorate, following the directions on page iii. Then transfer the same design to the felt. Using a small pair of very sharp scissors, carefully cut around the design. Pin the felt design to the garment and baste in place. Then, using a matching color sewing thread or embroidery floss, fasten the felt appliqué to the base material with small, even stitches.

18   Baranya and Bacsmegye

Bicske

This district is noted for an unusual form of decoration. Instead of being embroidered, the design is worked in soft, white cord appliqué. To duplicate this technique, first transfer the pattern as for embroidery. Start the cord on the wrong side of the fabric or garment you wish to decorate. Stitch the cord through the center at half-inch intervals, using white thread or floss and small, even stitches. Be sure to allow plenty of ease in the curves so that the cord lies smoothly. On completion, steam lightly on the wrong side on terry cloth towelling, using a damp cloth and a medium hot iron to raise the nap of the cord.

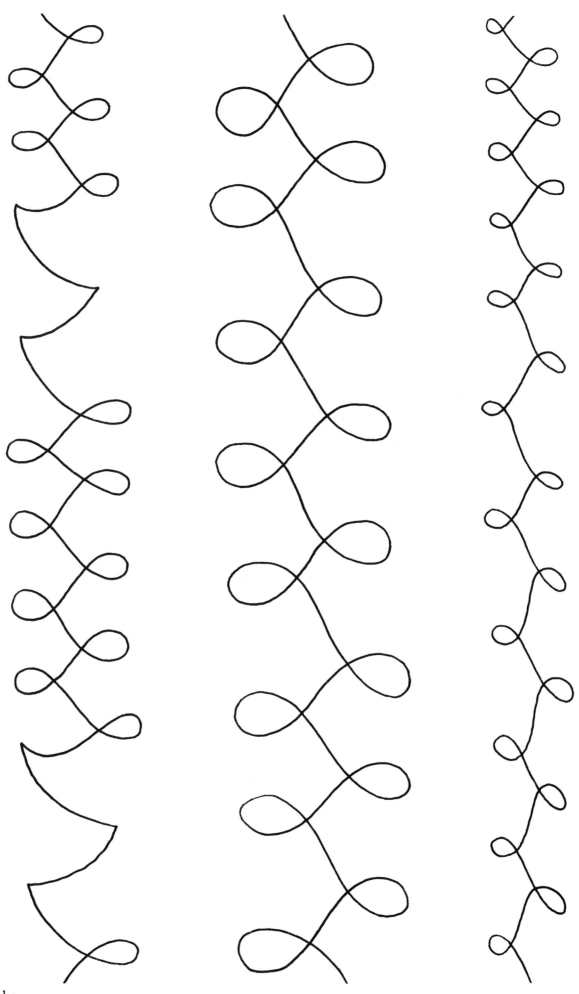

30 Bicske

Budapest

The Budapest folk art region includes Boldog, Csömör, Kerepes, Szada, Zsámbok, Kistarcsa, Nagytarcsa and Isaszegi. Many bright colors are suitable for working this district's flexible and variegated arrangements: blue, pink, orange, lovely shades of green, mauve, yellow—in short, all of the colors of the rainbow. Add a touch of black for drama or white for serenity. The Budapest region is also famous for its white-on-white work, and white on pastel-colored backgrounds. The designs in the Zsámbok area are usually worked in golden yellow floss on black, red or blue backgrounds.

Small, seed-shaped flower details are worked in lazy daisy stitch with petals and leaves in satin stitch. Running filling stitch is traditionally used for carnation petals and details. Stems, vines and outlines are worked in stem stitch, and satin stitch is used for the basic filled areas such as the flowers, buds and decorative dots around the flowers.

Drávaszög

Traditional embroidery of the craft area of Drávaszög uses many colors—shades of yellow, brown, red, grey and lavender with touches of black and white. Additional attractive color combinations include crimson or white floss on a brown background; steel blue on a white background, and white floss on a pastel background.

Stem and vine details are worked in stem and chain stitch. Flower center details are worked in a lazy daisy stitch with satin stitch for filling flower shapes, and buttonhole stitch for flowers with five, six or ten petals.

Hajdú-Bihar

Lots of stemwork and pretty floral designs characterize the embroidery from the Hajdú-Bihar area. Delicate white embroidery on white fabric is quite popular, and other traditional color schemes include red on a white background, golden yellow on medium brown, and sky-blue on terra cotta.

Basic rose shapes are traditionally worked in satin stitch, following the lines of the design. Satin stitch is also used for leaves, flowers, buds and flower centers. Stems and vines are worked in outline stitch with seed detail around the large flowers in lazy daisy stitch.

Kalocsa

The embroidery of Kalocsa is one of the most popular forms of folk art in Hungary. Traditionally, "writing women" painted the designs free-hand on the white background, and the women folk artists worked them in an endless and fascinating range of colors. Wall paintings are another outstanding folk art form rendered by these highly talented women who paint free-hand designs on the white-washed walls, filling the entire wall with elaborate designs.

Typical color combinations in embroidery are blue on a grey background, white on navy, or black on white—with an added touch of either hot pink or red. Another common color scheme uses different shades of a single color. Use the darkest shade for the center of the flower and make succeeding rows lighter and lighter as you work your way to the edge. If you plan to use this color scheme, there is actually only one rule to follow: observe the natural colors of the flowers and greenery.

Traditionally the embroidery is worked entirely in stem or outline for the stems and satin stitch for the other areas.

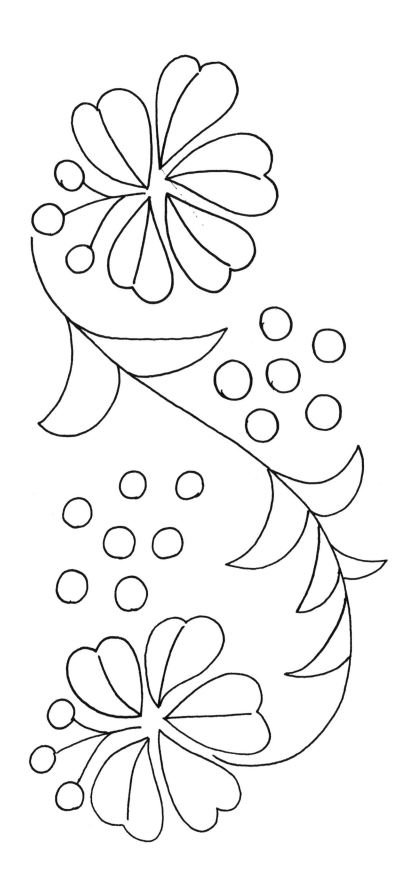

Karádi

Pastel designs worked on matching or contrasting backgrounds are characteristic of Karádi work. A combination of bright red berries and green leaves on a white or black background is also attractive and typical.

Long, leaf shapes are worked in lazy daisy stitches with stems and vines in outline stitch. Satin stitch is used for short, curved leaves, buds and flowers.

Matyó

Matyó embroidery, with its varied and colorful designs, has been extremely popular since the 1880s. It lends itself to innovations and bright, happy colors. In one typical color scheme, the background material is beige, white or grey; the flowers and larger leaves red; the flower centers and smaller leaves blue. Other attractive and lively color schemes use shades of one or two colors— such as light and dark green; light and dark red with medium blue; bright orange, wine and touches of white. Always be sure to use bright, fresh colors. The colors used in Matyó work are meant to symbolize elements of Hungarian life. Red represents joy, black the earth or soil, and blue death and grief.

Traditionally leaves and flowers are worked in satin stitch with stems, vines and decorative lines in stem stitch.

Sárköz

Sárköz embroidery has its origins in Byzantine culture. Brought to Hungary by the Turks, the Byzantine forms were gradually adapted by local folk artists. Many different colors are used for Sárköz embroidery. Combine a blue background with white embroidery, or work the motifs in white on a brown or yellow material. Black, beige, bright yellow, green, red and dark brown on matching or contrasting backgrounds also work well.

Chain stitch is traditionally used to outline flower centers and work circles. Vines, stems and other line work is done in outline stitch, and large areas (including some flower shapes) in split stitch.

94   Sárköz

Sióagárd

Stylized tulips, poppies and roses are the principal motifs in Sióagárd folk art. The background material is usually either medium yellow or beige and favorite colors for floss are maroon, medium pink, wine, light blue, red, olive and orange.

Designs are merely outlined on the fabric using stem stitch for flowers, buds, leaves and circles and outline stitch for stems, vines and other line work.

Turai

Pastels, especially blue, are definite favorites for Turai embroidery. Pointed leaves and pointed stylized flower petals are worked in lazy daisy stitch while the centers of flowers and the round flowers are worked in satin stitch. Assorted line work—such as stems and vines—is worked in stem stitch.

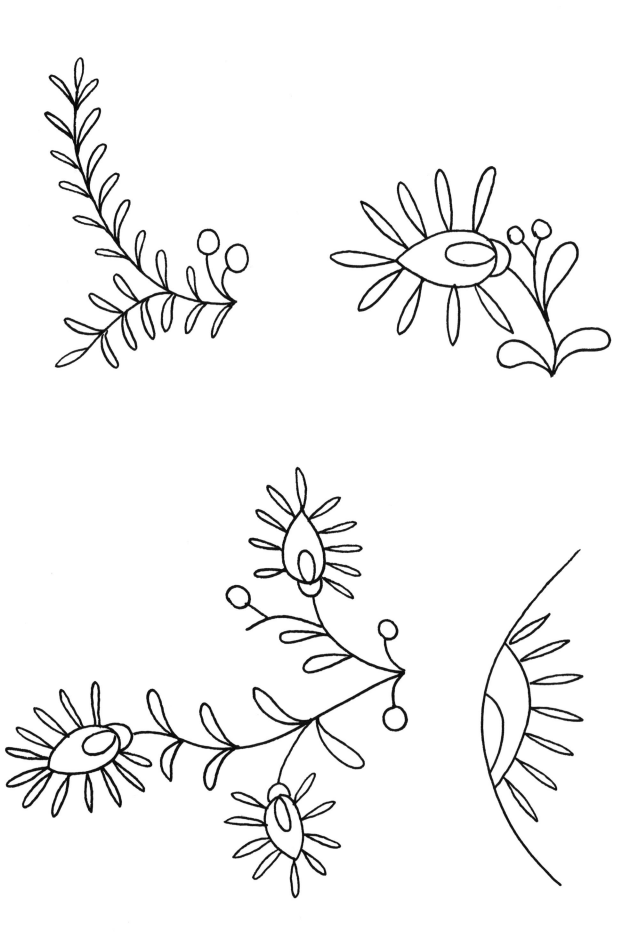

Zalai

To do a piece in the Zalai style, choose white or any pastel color for the background and work the entire design in pure white. Use satin stitch for star-shaped flowers, petal designs, circle decorations and larger, fuller leaves. Stems and other line work should be worked in stem stitch.